The Self-Care Reset for Black Women

Embrace Your Essence, Empower Your Journey

by Pamela Renee Gunn

Self-Care for Black Women: Embrace Your Essence, Empower Your Journey

Copyright © 2025 by Pamela Gunn

For permission requests, write to:

Expression Is Life, LLC

Email: expressionislifepublishing@gmail.com

Published by Expression Is Life Publishing

All rights reserved. Printed in the United States of America.

ISBN: 9798993568904

Cover Design by **Creative Chesta**@creativechesta8

Interior Design by Pamela Gunn

Scripture quotations are taken from The Holy Bible,
Amplified Version and The Message Bible.

Used by permission. All rights reserved.

This is a work of nonfiction. Any resemblance to actual
persons, living or dead, is purely coincidental.

First Edition — 2025

Dedication:

For every Black woman who has ever forgotten to rest —
this is your reminder to come home to yourself.

*May you remember, rest is righteous, and you are
worthy of it.*

Table of Contents

Author's Prologue

The Self Care Reset: For Black Women

by Pamela Gunn

This book is personal.

I didn't just decide to write about self-care — I needed to. It became a calling, a part of my own healing journey. Somewhere between being everything for everybody else and losing myself in the noise of busyness, I realized something: we glorify being busy, but we rarely honor the beauty of rest.

Growing up, I didn't have examples of women slowing down to take care of themselves first. I saw hard-working women — powerful, giving, resilient — but also tired, worn down, and constantly pouring from an empty cup. That's what I thought womanhood meant. That's what I thought strength looked like. But over time, I learned that exhaustion is not our birthright, and rest is not a reward — it's necessary.

One day, while talking with a friend about burnout, she asked a question that stopped me in my tracks:

"Do Black women even know when we're burnt out? Or do we just say we're tired?"

That question sat with me. Because for so long, "tired" has been our normal. We've carried the title Strong Black Woman like armor — and somewhere along the way, we started to believe it was all we were allowed to be. We were taught to survive, not to rest. To endure, not to exhale.

But I'm so thankful to see the shift happening — the rise of the soft girl era, the permission to take off the cape, the awareness that we deserve softness too. Still, for many of us, it's not easy to embrace. When you've lived your whole life in survival mode, peace can feel unfamiliar.

This book isn't about burnout. It's about avoiding it. It's about weaving self-care into your daily life — not as another task, but as a way of being. Because self-care isn't just bubble baths and candles (though those are nice). It's boundaries. It's breathing. It's listening when your body says rest.

The Self Care Reset is an invitation to slow down, reset, and rediscover yourself. It's for the woman who's been carrying it all — and is finally ready to put some things down. It's for the woman who's learning that choosing herself isn't selfish — it's sacred.

Because when Black women heal, when we rest, when we love ourselves out loud — the whole world shifts.

So take this moment. Inhale peace, exhale pressure. Let this be your reminder that you deserve to rest, to reset, and to rise again — softer, fuller, whole.

"Be still, and know that I am God."

— Psalm 46:10

Welcome to The Self Care Reset.
You're home now.

Introduction

Self-care is more than just a trend; it's a lifeline.

Sis, it's time.

For too long, we have poured from empty cups, showing up for everyone but ourselves. We carry the weight of expectations, the demands of family, careers, relationships, and the unspoken rule that as Black women, we must always be strong. But what happens when that strength begins to weigh us down?

I know this struggle firsthand. As a mother, wife, sister, and friend, I have worn many hats—sometimes too many. By my mid-thirties, I had just welcomed my second child, earned my MBA, and returned to school for a master's in education. I was climbing the corporate ladder, doing all the right things, yet inside, I felt empty. Depleted. Purposeless.

I was burnt out. And I wanted out.

I remember crying out to God, asking, "Is this it?" I reached a point where I begged for either a purpose or an escape from the exhaustion that had consumed me. That was my wake-up call.

This book is my love letter to you, my sister. In these pages, I share the self-care routines that restored—practices that bring balance, peace, and renewal to my mind, body, and soul. True self-care is more than a bubble bath or a spa day; it's about reclaiming our power, setting boundaries, and prioritizing our well-being unapologetically.

"Do not conform to the pattern of this world but be transformed by the renewing of your mind. Then you will be able to test and approve what God's will is—His good, pleasing and perfect will."
— Romans 12:2 (NIV)

Every day, we must renew our minds, letting go of stress, expectations, and exhaustion to embrace rest, healing, and divine alignment.

Journal Prompt:

What areas of your life feel out of balance right now? How can you begin to prioritize yourself without guilt?

Quote to Reflect On:

"Almost everything will work again if you unplug it for a few minutes, including you." — Anne Lamott

It's time to take self-care to the next level—not as a luxury, but as a necessity. You deserve it.

Let's begin.

Chapter 1: What Is Self-care, really?

Sis, let's talk.

For too long, self-care has been painted as a luxury, something extra, something you do if you have time, if you have money, or if everything else is done first. But here's the truth: self-care is not a luxury; it's a necessity. It's not about being selfish; it's about survival. It's about honoring yourself, raising your vibration, and showing up as your best self, for you first, and then for everyone else.

And the best part? Self-care doesn't have to be extravagant or expensive. It's not just spa days and tropical vacations (though, if that's your thing, go for it!). True self-care is about nourishing your body, mind, and spirit in ways that feel right for you.

Self-care Is Personal

What fuels your soul? What makes you feel whole? What are the simple things bring you peace?

Self-care looks different for everyone, and it should. Some women find it in prayer and meditation, others in journaling, movement, or simply sitting in silence with a cup of tea. It might be dancing to your favorite song, walking barefoot in the grass, or turning off your phone for a few hours. Whatever it is, it should feel like coming home to yourself.

Breaking Free from the "Strong Black Woman" Narrative

Let's be real, too often, as Black women, we're expected to carry the world on our backs. We're mothers, wives, sisters, caregivers, professionals, and the ones everyone leans on. We're told to be strong, to push through, to sacrifice. But at what cost?

Self-care starts with giving yourself permission to slow down. To say no without guilt. To rest. To acknowledge when you're tired, mentally drained, or emotionally depleted. You do not have to earn rest, you deserve it. And when you take care of yourself, you set the standard for how others should treat you, too.

Setting Boundaries Is Self-care

One of the biggest acts of self-care? Learning to say "no."

We've been conditioned to believe that our worth is tied to how much we do for others. But sis, let me tell you something, your worth is not measured by your productivity. You don't have to overextend yourself to be valuable. It's okay to set boundaries. It's okay to protect your energy. It's okay to choose yourself first.

Boundaries might mean saying no to obligations that drain you, turning down invitations when you need rest, or limiting your availability to people who take more than they give. When you establish boundaries, you're not pushing people away, you're creating space for your peace.

Find What Sparks Joy and Do More of It

Self-care isn't complicated. It's the little things that bring you joy, things that feel good to your soul.

Maybe it's reading a good book, taking a long walk, cooking your favorite meal, or dancing in your living room. Maybe it's morning prayer, listening to music, or just sitting in stillness and breathing. Self-care is simply doing what makes you feel alive.

The key is to be intentional. Prioritize yourself the way you prioritize everything and everyone else.

Self-care Is a Movement, not a Moment

Taking care of yourself is not a one-time thing. It's not something you squeeze in when you have "extra" time. It's a lifestyle.

And we don't have to do it alone. As we embrace self-care, we should uplift and support one another. When Black women prioritize their well-being, we create a ripple effect, one that heals, restores, and empowers generations to come.

So, let this be your reminder: you deserve peace, joy, and balance. You deserve to pour into yourself the way you pour into others.

Journal Prompt:

What does self-care mean to you? List three things you can do this week to nourish your mind, body, and spirit.

Quote to Reflect On:

"Caring for myself is not self-indulgence, it is self-preservation, and that is an act of political warfare."- Audre Lorde

Sis, it's time to put yourself first. You are worthy. You are enough. Let's start this journey together.

Chapter 2: The Moment, I Chose Myself

For years, I was running on empty.

I AM a mother, a wife, a manager, and a woman juggling every role imaginable, except the role of being present for myself. I was overworked, and overwhelmed. My health was slipping, my energy was gone, and when I looked in the mirror, I didn't recognize the woman staring back at me. I had let myself go, not just physically, but mentally and emotionally.

I told myself; this is just life.
I told myself; this is what being a strong woman looks like.
I told myself; I don't have time for self-care right now.

But one day, I sat down with my journal, something I had barely touched in months, and wrote a simple question:

"What did you do today to honor yourself?"

And I had no answer.

I could tell you what I did for my kids, how I showed up for my husband, how I poured into my team at work. But when it came to me? I had nothing. That was my wake-up call. Something had to change.

Choosing Myself Was Not Selfish-It Was Necessary

I started small. I made time to move my body, not to lose weight, but to feel good in my skin. I started eating better, not to chase a number on the scale, but to fuel myself with love. I carved out quiet moments just for me, whether that was sipping my tea in silence, taking deep breaths before diving into the chaos of the day, or writing in my journal at night.

And as I did, something shifted.

I stopped feeling guilty for resting.
I stopped believing that my worth was tied to how much I could do for others.
I stopped neglecting the one person who needed me the most-ME.

The Power of Reflection

That journaling prompt, "What did you do today to honor yourself?", became my daily check-in. At first, I struggled to find an answer. But with time, I started filling those pages with simple yet powerful acts of self-love.

"I took a 10-minute walk and breathed in fresh air."
"I said no to something that didn't serve me."
"I played my favorite song and danced in my kitchen."
"I gave myself permission to just be."

Each time I wrote something down, I reclaimed a little bit of myself.

This Is Your Reminder, Sis

If you're reading this and feeling like you've been pouring from an empty cup, I see you. I was you. And I want you to know that you are allowed to take care of yourself.

You don't need permission to rest.
You don't have to earn self-care.
You don't have to keep putting yourself last.

I made the choice to put me back on my priority list, and my life changed for the better. Now, I invite you to do the same.

Journal Prompt:

"At the end of today, what will you have done to honor yourself?"

Quote to Reflect On:

"Almost everything will work again if you unplug it for a few minutes, including you."- Anne Lamott

It's time to unplug, reset, and choose you.

Chapter 3: Dating Myself, The Ultimate Self-care Routine

For the longest time, I waited. I waited for friends to be available. I waited for someone to invite me out. I waited for a reason to celebrate. And then I realized, *I am the reason*.

One of the most powerful self-care practices I learned to do is dating myself. Yes, you heard that right. I take myself out on dates, and I don't wait for company. Because if I'm not comfortable spending time with me, what makes me think others will be comfortable in my presence?

Why Dating Yourself is a Game-Changer

Spending time alone isn't lonely, it's liberating. It gives you a chance to learn more about yourself, what you like, and what truly makes you happy. It helps you build confidence, independence, and an unshakable sense of self-worth. Plus, you never know who you might meet when you're out enjoying life on your own terms.

My Favorite Self-Date Ritual

Once a week, I schedule time just for me. I get dressed up not for anyone else, but for myself. I get my make-up done, put on an outfit that makes me feel beautiful, and I show up for me.

My favorite solo date? Social hour at my favorite bar or restaurant. I sit at the bar, order my favorite cocktail, and simply enjoy the moment. No distractions, no obligations, just me, treating myself with the same energy I'd want someone else to.

This time isn't about waiting for someone to validate me. It's about celebrating myself, whether there's something big to celebrate or just the fact that I made it through the week.

Why Some Women Find This Taboo

It's funny, whenever I tell women that I date myself, I often get the same reaction:
"I could never do that!"
"That feels so uncomfortable!"
"I would feel weird sitting alone!"

But why? Why do we feel uncomfortable showing up for ourselves?

The truth is, society teaches women, especially Black women, to always be in service to others. We give so much to our families, our jobs, and our relationships that we forget how to just be with ourselves.

But dating yourself isn't just for single women. Whether you're married, in a relationship, or enjoying your single season, making time for yourself is essential.

How to Start Dating Yourself

Pick a place you enjoy. Coffee shops, restaurants, museums, bookstores, or even the park, go where you feel good.

Dress up for YOU. Wear what makes you feel confident and beautiful.

Be present. Put your phone down. Take in your surroundings. Enjoy your meal, sip your drink, and embrace the moment.

Remember that you deserve this. You don't need an occasion or permission to treat yourself well.

Journal Prompt:

"What is one place you've always wanted to go alone but never have? How would it feel to show up for yourself?"

Quote to Reflect On:

"Loving yourself isn't vanity. It's sanity."-Katrina Mayer

Sis, it's time to stop waiting. Show up for yourself, date yourself, and fall in love with the woman you are becoming.

Chapter 4: Creating: The Art of Expression

They say the antidote to depression is expression, and I couldn't agree more.

For me, self-care isn't just about bubble baths and spa days, it's about creating. It's about letting what's inside of me flow freely, without restriction, without fear. Ever since I was a little girl, I've found solace in writing. Whether it was journaling, writing songs, or crafting short stories, I've always turned to words to make sense of my emotions, my experiences, and my purpose.

Creativity as an Outlet for Healing

I have hundreds of journals. Seriously, hundreds. Each one tells a story, some personal, some poetic, some raw and unfiltered. My journals become songs. My songs become books. And through it all, I heal.

I don't believe in withholding anything. I believe in expressing myself. I believe in pouring out, releasing, and sharing because there is power in creativity. It's the way I process life. When I feel overwhelmed, I write. When I feel lost, I write. When I need clarity, I write.

And they overcame...by the word of their testimony... Revelation 12:11 (KJV)

This scripture reminds me that our stories have power. The more we speak, write, and share our experiences, the more we heal, not just ourselves, but others.

Dying Empty: Leaving Nothing Behind

One of my favorite sayings is:
"I want to die empty."

That may sound heavy, but to me, it means living fully. It means that whatever God has placed inside of me, I want to express it, share it, and give it away before I leave this side of the plane. I don't want to take my songs, my stories, or my ideas to the grave. I want to release them into the world while I'm here to witness their impact.

Journaling as Self-care

Journaling is therapeutic. I keep a journal next to my bed, and it holds my deepest thoughts, my conversations with God, my reflections on life. Some days, I write my prayers. I will write about my dreams. And when I look back, I see growth. I see healing. I see me.

Writing isn't just a hobby, it's a form of self-care that allows me to slow down, reflect, and create meaning in my life.

How You Can Tap into Your Creativity

You don't have to be a writer to create. Creativity shows up in different forms, painting, dancing, singing, cooking, decorating, designing, or even speaking. Find what lights you up and make space for it.

Keep a journal by your bed and write for 5 minutes before sleeping.

Create something, whether it's a poem, a vision board, or a doodle.

Give yourself permission to express yourself freely, without judgment.

Journal Prompt:

"What is something creative that brings you joy, and how can you make more time for it?"

Quote to Reflect On:

"Creativity is the way I share my soul with the world."-Brené Brown

Sis, create your way to healing. Don't hold back. Your testimony, your gifts, your creativity, they are meant to be shared. The world needs what's inside of you.

Chapter 5: Solo Travel, Healing Through Exploration

There's something powerful about packing a bag, setting out on a journey, and discovering the world on your own terms.

Solo travel has become one of my favorite self-care routines. It's not just about going to new places, it's about gaining new perspectives, stepping outside of my comfort zone, and allowing myself the space to breathe, reflect, and heal.

For years, I waited for friends, family, or a partner to be available before I took certain trips. But one day, I decided enough was enough. I wasn't going to put my experiences on hold for the sake of companionship. So, I started booking trips for myself, whether it was a simple day trip, a weekend getaway, or an extended vacation. And let me tell you, it changed everything.

The Healing Power of Solo Travel

Traveling alone forces you to be present. There's no one else to set the itinerary. No one to compromise with. Just you and the adventure ahead. And in that space, you learn yourself in ways you never could in your daily routine.

You learn what excites you. You learn how to enjoy your own company. You learn that solitude is not loneliness, it's liberation. For me, solo travel became a way to reconnect with my soul.

Finding Freedom While Working Remotely

One of the biggest blessings in my journey was realizing that I could travel while still working remotely. This discovery changed everything for me! I no longer had to wait for vacation days to explore the world, I could take my laptop and go.

Traveling allowed me to see that the world was my oyster, and there was so much beyond what the eye can see. It shifted my mindset and expanded my vision. I realized that many people live their entire lives in one place out of fear, never stepping beyond what's familiar. But what I have come to learn is this: sometimes your assignment is outside of your comfort zone.

Discovering My Love for Mountains

Through my travels, I learned something new about myself, I am an orophile (a lover of mountains). There is something about being surrounded by towering peaks that makes me feel connected to something greater than myself. Mountains remind me that life is about elevation, about rising above challenges and reaching new heights.

A Life, Changing Trip to Africa

In 2022, I took a trip to Africa, and that experience unlocked something deep within me. I realized that up until that point, I had barely scratched the surface of what this world had to offer. The culture, the landscapes, the people, it was all so vibrant, so full of life. That trip ignited a knack for travel that I never knew I had.

I returned home with a renewed sense of purpose. I understood that my journey was about more than just self-care, it was about discovery, about pushing past limitations, and about embracing every opportunity that life had to offer.

My Favorite Solo Travel Destinations

One of the most beautiful places I've ever visited was Sedona, Arizona. There's a spiritual energy there that's undeniable. The red rocks, the open sky, the healing vortices, it's a place that truly grounds you. I remember standing at the edge of a cliff, looking out over the landscape, and feeling an overwhelming sense of peace. It was as if the land itself was whispering, you are exactly where you need to be.

Another favorite destination of mine is San Diego, California. Something about the mix of beaches and hiking trails just speaks to my spirit. I love nothing more than walking along the coast, letting the ocean breeze wash away any stress I might be holding. It's a reminder that nature is one of the greatest healers we have.

One of the most soothing ways I love to travel is by train. There's something about watching the world pass by through a train window that is deeply therapeutic. One of my favorite train rides is along a scenic coast, where the ocean meets the land, and I can just sit back, sip, and be.

How Solo Travel Transformed Me

Solo travel is more than just a vacation; it's a self-care practice. It teaches you to be comfortable in your own presence, to trust yourself, and to embrace the unknown. It's healing. It's freedom. If you've never traveled alone, I encourage you to start small: Take a day trip to a nearby town. Treat yourself to a solo staycation at a hotel. Book a train ride and just enjoy the journey.

You don't have to go far to experience the benefits. The goal is to step outside of routine and give yourself the gift of exploration.

Journal Prompt:

"If you could take a solo trip anywhere in the world, where would you go and why?"

Quote to Reflect On:

"Traveling solo does not always mean you're alone. Most often, you meet incredible people along the way and make connections that last a lifetime.", -Unknown

Sis, book the trip. Take the train. Go see the world. You deserve it.

Chapter 6: Girlfriend Therapy, The Power of Sisterhood

I always say, we need a community of sisterhood! Life wasn't meant to be walked alone, and as women, we thrive in connection. It's not about competition; it's about community. We pour so much into our families, our work, and our responsibilities, but who pours into us? That's where girlfriend therapy comes in.

The Necessity of Girlfriend Therapy

One of the most powerful self-care routines I've incorporated into my life is scheduling intentional time with my sisters and friends. Whether it's over brunch, a phone call, or a weekend getaway, these moments of connection are essential for my emotional and mental well-being. It's a safe space where we can share our struggles, celebrate our wins, and remind each other who we are.

If you are blessed to have a solid community of women in your life, you know just how life giving it is.

It's a space to be heard without judgment. It's a place to laugh until you cry and heal through shared experiences. It's an opportunity to pour into one another, because as much as we give, we need to receive, too.

The Power of Women Coming Together

Historically, women have gathered in community. There was a time when we would come together during our cycles, creating sacred spaces for rest, renewal, and wisdom, sharing. When the men were out in the fields working, the women took care of not just their households but each other. They raised children together, cooked together, and supported one another in a way that made the burden of life feel lighter.

I truly believe that in today's world, this sense of sisterhood is just as important, if not more. With the demands of modern life pulling us in a thousand directions, we need to be intentional about nurturing our relationships with other women.

Making Sisterhood a Self-care Practice

For me, girlfriend therapy isn't just a "nice-to-have." It's a must. I make it a practice to schedule meetups with my closest friends, just like I would a doctor's appointment or a business meeting. It's that important.

Some of my favorite ways to connect with my sisterhood include:

Sunday brunches filled with laughter and real talk.

Group chats where we hype each other up, send daily affirmations, or just check in.

Girls' trips to refresh, recharge, and make new memories.

Wellness dates, spa days, hiking trips, or even a simple walk in the park together.

Because here's the thing: life is heavy sometimes. And as much as we like to think we can carry it all on our own, we're not meant to. God created us for community.

Sisterhood as Healing

I have found that my most healing conversations have been with my girlfriends. The moments when I felt like I couldn't go on, they reminded me of my strength. When I forgot who I was, they held up a mirror and showed me the queen

I am. They've wiped my tears, prayed over me, and challenged me to be better.

So, if you don't already have a community of sisterhood, I encourage you to start cultivating one. Reach out to women you trust, invest in deep and meaningful friendships, and make girlfriend therapy a priority.

Because we all need a space where we can take off the superwoman cape, let our guards down, and simply be.

Journal Prompt:

"Who are the women in my life who pour into me? How can I be more intentional about nurturing those relationships?"

Quote to Reflect On:

"Behind every successful woman is a tribe of other successful women who have her back."

Sis, call your girls. Make the plan. Create the space. Because you deserve it.

Chapter 7: The Sacred Ritual of a Spiritual Bath

Self-care isn't just about the external, it's about nurturing the soul. One of my favorite self-care rituals is indulging in a spiritual bath, something I make time for at least twice a month. This isn't just any ordinary soak in the tub. It's a sacred experience, an intentional moment to unwind, reflect, and reconnect with myself.

A Ritual Fit for a Queen

In the Bible, we see that queens prepared themselves with intentional beauty and cleansing rituals. Queen Esther, before she was presented to the king, went through a full year of beauty treatment six months with oil of myrrh and six months with perfumes and cosmetics.

"Before a young woman's turn came to go into King Xerxes, she had to complete twelve months of beauty treatments prescribed for the women, six months with oil of myrrh and six with perfumes and cosmetics."
-Esther 2:12 (NIV)

Esther's preparation wasn't just about physical beauty, it was about spiritual refinement and readiness. Similarly, my spiritual bath is a time of purification, not just externally but internally, a moment to release, reset, and restore my energy.

The Goddess Bath

A Goddess Bath is a special bath infused with a blend of herbs and flowers and oils or whatever speaks to you. It's a blend of flower petals, essential oils, Epsom salts, and Himalayan salt. You can add other elements such as candles and aromatherapy, depending on your intentions.

This bath is designed to:
🌿 Cleanse your aura – Washing away negativity and stagnant energy
🌸 Fully relax – Releasing tension and stress from the body
🪶 Connect with your Divine Feminine and Goddess Energy – Tapping into your intuition, self-love, and inner power

A great basic ritual bath to start with includes:

Rose petals – Symbolizes love, healing, and beauty

Lavender oil – Known for its calming and soothing effects

Epsom salts – Helps detox the body and ease muscle tension

Pink Himalayan salt – Aids in purification and energy clearing

"I will sprinkle clean water on you, and you will be clean; I will cleanse you from all your impurities and from all your idols."
- Ezekiel 36:25 (NIV)

"He saved us through the washing of rebirth and renewal by the Holy Spirit."
-Titus 3:5 (NIV)

Setting the Atmosphere

A spiritual bath is all about intention. I don't just run hot water and jump in, I create an experience.

Here's how I prepare:

Candles: Soft, warm lighting sets the mood and brings a sense of peace.

Music: I choose soothing sounds, whether it's worship music, R&B, or the calming sound of ocean waves.

Herbs & Flowers: Depending on my intention, I add elements such as chamomile for peace, rosemary for protection, or jasmine for intuition.

Affirmations & Prayer: I use this time to speak life over myself, meditate, or simply be still.

As I soak, I allow myself to let go. I reflect on my achievements, my struggles, and everything I've overcome. It's a time to celebrate myself or simply release whatever no longer serves me.

Why a Spiritual Bath is a Must

It's my time to reset, recharge, and realign. When I skip it, I feel it. My mind feels cluttered, my energy feels drained, and I know it's time to pause and pour back into myself.

Sis, if you haven't incorporated spiritual baths into your self-care routine, I encourage you to try it. Set the mood, be intentional, and allow yourself to simply be.

Journal Prompt:

"What is something I need to release before stepping into my next season?"

Affirmation

"I give myself permission to rest, to release, and to recharge. I am worthy of peace."

Take the time to pour into yourself. You deserve it.

Chapter 8: The Sacred Ritual of Skincare

Skincare isn't just about having clear skin; it's about nourishing yourself inside and out. For me, skincare has become a self-care ritual, a moment where I pause, breathe, and pour back into myself. It's not just about the products I use; it's about the intention behind it.

Rewriting the Narrative

Growing up, skincare wasn't emphasized as a priority. It wasn't something I was taught to cherish or incorporate into my daily life. But as I got older, I realized that taking care of my skin is an act of self-love. It's a time for me to slow down, check in with myself, and honor my body.

My Skincare Ritual

Each night, I set aside time to pamper myself with a full skincare routine. Here's what it looks like:

Cleansing – Washing away the stress of the day and releasing negativity

Exfoliating – Removing dead skin cells and making room for renewal (2-3x per week)

Serums & Treatments – Hydrating and

nourishing my skin with love

🌿 Masking – A deeper level of care, depending on what my skin needs (2,3x per week)

💧 Moisturizing – Locking in hydration and sealing in all the goodness

Mirror Talk & Affirmations

What makes my skincare routine special is what I say to myself while doing it. As I look in the mirror, I use this time to speak life into myself.

I affirm:

💜 "I am beautiful, inside and out."

💜 "My skin is glowing, and so is my spirit."

💜 "I honor myself by taking care of me."

💜 "I am worthy of love, care, and peace."

Instead of criticizing myself in the mirror, I have learned to celebrate myself. It's a time to be naked and honest with myself. This shift in mindset has been transformational, not just for my skin but for my self-esteem and self-worth.

The Power of Touch & Self-Love

There's something powerful about caring for yourself with your own hands. Each time I apply a moisturizer or a mask, it's not just about skincare, it's a gentle reminder that I am worthy of care and love.

Having a skincare routine isn't just about having glowing skin. It's about creating moments of self-care and affirmation, reminding myself that I deserve to be nurtured, by me, for me.

Journal Prompt:

"How can I incorporate more self-love into my daily routine?"

Affirmation:

"I am radiant. I am worthy. I am enough."

Skincare is self-care. Take the time to honor yourself, every single day.

Chapter 9: Reconnecting with Nature & Digital Detox

In a world that never seems to slow down, I have learned that stepping away and reconnecting with nature is one of the most powerful forms of self-care. There is something deeply healing about walking among the trees, feeling the sun on my skin, and breathing in the fresh air. Nature is my reset button.

The Healing Power of Nature Walks

I make it a practice to take regular walks in nature, not just for the physical benefits but for my mental and emotional well-being. When I walk, I allow myself to:

🌿 Reconnect with the Earth – Feeling grounded and present in the moment

🍃 Breathe Fresh Air – Cleansing my mind from stress and overwhelm

😊 Absorb Natural Energy – Letting the sun recharge my spirit

☁️ Clear My Mind – Creating space for new ideas and peaceful thoughts

Some of my favorite places to take nature walks include:

🏞 Parks with open green spaces

🌊 Beaches where I can listen to the waves

🌲 Forest trails where I feel surrounded by peace

During these walks, I often use the time to pray, meditate, or simply be still. I let go of the pressures of the day and focus on the simple joys, the rustling leaves, the singing birds, the way the earth feels beneath my feet.

The Power of a Digital Detox

Another essential part of my self-care practice is unplugging from technology. We live in a world where we are constantly connected, scrolling, answering messages, and being bombarded with information. But I have come to realize that true peace comes from within, not from a screen.

I set aside intentional time for a digital detox, where I:

📵 Turn off notifications

📖 Read a book or journal

🧘 Meditate and focus on my breath

♡ Spend uninterrupted time with myself and loved ones

Taking these breaks allows me to be fully present. I no longer feel the need to be accessible 24/7, instead, I focus on being in tune with myself.

Journal Prompt:

"How do I feel when I disconnect from technology and reconnect with nature?"

Affirmation:

"I honor myself by taking time to unplug, reset, and reconnect with the world around me."

Nature walks and digital detoxing have taught me that peace isn't found in a screen, it's found in stillness, in presence, and in the beauty of the world around us.

Chapter 10: Gardening & The Joy of Growth

There is something incredibly therapeutic about planting a seed, nurturing it, and watching it grow. Gardening has become one of my most rewarding self-care practices reminders that growth takes time, patience, and love.

The Healing Power of Gardening

I have developed a deep love for seeing things grow, whether they're fresh herbs in my kitchen, vibrant flowers in my yard, or vegetables in my garden. It does something to me mentally. The act of planting, watering, and tending to my garden is a form of meditation, a time for me to be fully present.

🌱 Gardening teaches me patience. Just like in life, growth doesn't happen overnight. Every plant requires care, the right conditions, and time to bloom.

🌿 It reminds me to nurture myself. If I can pour love and energy into my plants, I must do the same for myself.

🍎 It brings the joy of harvest. There is something powerful about reaping what I have sown, both in my garden and in my life.

Creating a Homestead & Harvest Parties

I am working on creating a homestead, a space where I can grow my own food, live more sustainably, and celebrate the beauty of nature. One of my biggest dreams is to host harvest parties, gathering loved ones to enjoy the fruits of our labor, cooking meals with fresh ingredients, and celebrating the simple joys of life.

Gardening isn't just about growing plants; it's about growing myself. It teaches me resilience, the beauty of cycles, and the importance of nurturing what matters most. This is self-care.

Journal Prompt:

"What is something I have nurtured and watched grow in my life?"

Affirmation:

"I honor my growth, just as I honor the growth of the world around me."

Whether it's tending to a garden, caring for houseplants, or simply appreciating nature's beauty, gardening is a reminder that growth is a journey, and it's always worth it.

Chapter 11: The Power of Breathwork

Breathing, something so simple, yet so powerful. Breathwork has become one of my most essential self-care routines because it allows me to quiet my mind, ease anxiety, and bring myself back to the present moment.

Why Breathwork?

For a long time, I didn't realize how often I held my breath throughout the day, especially during stressful moments. I was constantly moving, giving, working, but rarely pausing. I didn't understand that something as simple as intentional breathing could help me manage stress, increase focus, and bring a sense of calm to my daily life.

My Daily Breathwork Practice

Each day, I take at least 10 minutes to focus on my breath. Whether it's in the morning before I start my day or at night to unwind, this practice helps me:

- Calm my anxious thoughts
- Reset my nervous system

- Find clarity and focus
- Feel more grounded and present

One of my favorite techniques is the 4,4,4 breathing method:

Inhale deeply for 4 seconds

Hold the breath for 4 seconds

Exhale slowly for 4 seconds

Repeat for a few rounds

This simple practice helps me release tension and reset my mind.

The Spiritual Connection

Breath is life. The breath is a gift from YAHWEH, a reminder of our connection to the Divine. In Genesis 2:7, it says:
"Then the Lord God formed man of dust from the ground and breathed into his nostrils the breath of life, and the man became a living soul."

Breath is sacred. When I engage in breathwork, I feel as though I am aligning myself with God's peace, wisdom, and presence.

Journal Prompt:

"How does my breath feel in this moment? What emotions am I holding onto that I can release with each exhale?

Affirmation:

"With every breath, I invite peace, clarity, and divine alignment into my life."

Breathwork is more than just practice, it's a daily act of self-care that reminds me to slow down, be present, and honor my well-being.

Chapter 12: The Healing Power of Grounding

One of my favorite self-care routines is grounding, also known as earthing, the simple yet powerful practice of placing my bare feet directly on the earth. I first learned about earthing through a book, and it completely changed the way I connect with nature.

What is Grounding?

Grounding is the act of physically connecting with the earth's natural energy. Walking barefoot on grass, sand, or soil allows us to absorb the Earth's electromagnetic field, which can help reduce stress, improve sleep, and even decrease inflammation in the body.

Why I Love Grounding

I love the spring and summer months because they give me the perfect opportunity to walk barefoot, sit in the grass, and absorb the energy of nature. One of my favorite things to do is have a picnic in the yard, just me, a book, fresh fruit, and the warmth of the sun. There's something incredibly healing about sinking my feet into the earth, feeling the grass between my toes, and just being present.

The Science & Spirituality of Grounding

Studies have shown that grounding can:
- Reduce stress and anxiety
- Improve circulation and energy levels
- Promote better sleep
- Decrease pain and inflammation

But beyond the science, I believe grounding is a spiritual practice. It reminds me to slow down and be fully present in my body. Psalm 24:1 says:
"The earth is the Lord's, and everything in it, the world, and all who live in it."

When I ground myself, I feel connected, to God, to creation, and to my own being.

Journal Prompt:

"When was the last time I intentionally connected with nature? How did it make me feel?"

Affirmation:

"I am rooted, I am grounded, I am one with the earth and the divine energy that sustains me."

Grounding has become more than just a self-care ritual, it is a sacred practice that nourishes my mind, body, and soul.

Chapter 13: Creating a Morning Routine

Mornings set the tone for the day, and I have learned that starting my day with intention makes all the difference. One of the most important self-care routines I've adopted is creating a morning routine that nourishes my mind, body, and spirit.

Why Morning Routine Matters

For years, I would wake up and immediately jump into the demands of the day, rushing to work, tending to my family, and checking my phone before I even had a moment to breathe. I felt scattered, anxious, and reactive instead of centered and at peace. That changed when I started prioritizing intentional mornings.

My Morning Routine

Every morning, I dedicate at least 15 minutes to myself before the world starts pulling at me. Here's what my routine looks like:

Morning Prayer & Gratitude – I start my day by thanking God for another opportunity to live, grow, and experience life. Prayer sets the foundation for my day. Lamentations 3:22,23 reminds me:

"The steadfast love of the Lord never ceases; His mercies never come to an end; they are new every morning."

🧘 Meditation & Stillness – Before reaching for my phone or jumping into work, I take a few moments to sit in silence, breathe deeply, and set my intentions for the day.

📖 Reading & Reflection – Whether it's a passage from the Bible, a devotional, or an inspirational book, I spend a few minutes feeding my mind and spirit with wisdom.

☕ Tea or Coffee time – I love making a warm cup of tea or coffee and simply enjoying the moment, no rushing, no distractions.

The Power of Intentional Mornings

Starting my day calm, grounded, and focused has transformed my life. I am no longer reacting to life; I am setting the intention for how I want my day to unfold.

Journal Prompt:

"How can I create a morning routine that supports my well-being? What small habit can I add to my mornings?"

Affirmation:

"Each morning, I create space for peace, clarity, and gratitude. My day begins with purpose."

A morning routine doesn't have to be long or complicated. All it takes is a few intentional moments to set the tone for a beautiful and fulfilling day.

Chapter 14: The Power of Completion in Self-care

Self-care is not just about pampering ourselves; it's about honoring our commitments to ourselves. One of the most important lessons I've learned on this journey is that completion is self-care. When I set small, intentional goals and follow through, I build confidence, self-respect, and momentum in my life.

Setting Daily Goals to Honor Yourself

Each day, I set a goal, big or small, that is solely for me. It could be something as simple as:

💧 Drinking a gallon of water for hydration and wellness

🏋️ Making it to the gym for movement and strength

📚 Learning something new, reading, taking a course, or attending a workshop

🎨 Completing a creative project like a DIY vision board or prayer board

💌 Writing myself a letter of encouragement

🧘 Practicing mindfulness or meditation

🎭 Trying a new hobby that brings me joy

The Self-care Jar: A Fun Way to Prioritize You

One of my favorite self-care tools is my Self-care Jar. I fill it with different self-care activities written on small pieces of paper. Whenever I need a pick-me-up, I randomly select one and commit to doing it. Some ideas include:

- Take a 30, minute nap
- Buy yourself flowers
- Enjoy a long bath with candles
- Go for a scenic walk
- Watch a feel good movie
- Unplug from social media for the day

Completion as Self-care

Following through on self-care commitments is an act of self-love. When we complete even the smallest goals, we show ourselves that we are worthy of time, effort, and care.

Journal Prompt:

"What is one small goal I can complete today that will make me feel proud of myself?"

Affirmation:

"I honor myself by completing what I set out to do. Every small step I take is an act of self-love."

Self-care is a lifelong journey, and it starts with showing up for yourself, one completed goal at a time.

Final Chapter: The Power of Self-care

Self-care is not a luxury; it is a necessity. It is the foundation of self-love, healing, and personal growth. Through this journey, I have learned that prioritizing myself is not selfish; it is essential.

For too long, I placed myself on the back burner, pouring into everyone around me, my family, my career, my responsibilities, until I was running empty. I was overworked, underpaid, exhausted, and disconnected from myself. It wasn't until I made the intentional decision to change my narrative that I began to truly live.

Transformation Through Self-care

By committing to daily self-care routines, I rediscovered my strength, my joy, and my purpose. Whether it was journaling to reflect on my journey, dating myself to celebrate my existence, creating to express my soul, traveling to expand my mind, or grounding myself in nature, every act of self-care brought me closer to the best version of myself.

Self-care has taught me that:
🩶 I am worthy of my own time and attention.

💜 My well-being is just as important as the people I care for.

💜 When I pour into myself, I have more to give to others.

💜 Completion is self-care, honoring commitments to myself builds self-trust.

💜 Balance is key, rest is just as valuable as productivity.

A Call to Action: Choose You

As you have walked through this journey with me, I hope you have been inspired to make self-care a priority in your own life. I challenge you to start today, whether it's setting a goal, indulging in a self-care ritual, or simply giving yourself permission to rest.

Your self-care does not have to look like mine. Find what nourishes your soul, what brings you peace, what makes you feel alive, and commit to it.

And Don't Forget to Dance!

One of the most freeing forms of self-care is movement. Dance like nobody's watching, move your body, feel the rhythm of life, and let go of anything weighing you down. Dancing is a celebration of existence, and you deserve to celebrate yourself daily.

Final Journal Prompt:

"What is one self-care ritual I can commit to starting today?"

Affirmation:

"I honor myself daily. My self-care is a reflection of my self-love."

Self-care is a journey, not a destination. Every small act of love you give yourself is a step toward wholeness.

About the Author

Pamela Gunn is an author, educator, and singer-songwriter whose passion lies in helping others discover healing through the art of expression. With nearly 20 years of experience in the field of education and a master's in education, Pamela currently serves as a Special Education Teacher, where she advocates for inclusivity, creativity, and self-care among students and colleagues alike.

As the founder of *Expression Is Life Publishing*, Pamela empowers others to tell their stories by offering coaching, manuscript development, and publishing support. Writing, for her, is more than a craft, it's a calling rooted in faith, resilience, and purpose.

Her debut work, *Self-Care for Black Women: Embrace Your Essence, Empower Your Journey* is the first in a three-part series exploring self-care and wellness, especially for women who give so much of themselves to others.

Outside the classroom or recording in the studio, Pamela finds joy in music and performance. Whether on stage or at home with her loving family, she lives her life by her personal mantra: *Handle it with Equanimity*, a reminder to approach life's challenges with peace, balance, and grace.

www.ingramcontent.com/pod-product-compliance
Lightning Source LLC
Chambersburg PA
CBHW060416050426
42449CB00009B/1985